The MOMS' Truth

Authentic Stories of Motherhood

Stories Compiled by
PATRICE STERLING

Copyright © 2022

Authored and Compiled by

Patrice Sterling

All rights reserved. This book or parts thereof may not be reproduced in any form, stored in any retrieval system, or transmitted in any form by any means—electronic, mechanical, photocopy, recording, or otherwise—without prior written permission of the publisher, except as provided by United States of America copyright law. For permission requests, contact the publisher: info@patricesterling.com

First hardcover edition September 2022

Cover design by Josiah Abraham

ISBN 979-8-218-05751-0

Patrice Sterling Unlimited

Disclaimer

This book is a work of creative non-fiction. The stories and events portrayed within it are true; however, some details were changed to protect the privacy of those involved.

Further, the ideas, suggestions, and procedures provided in this book are not intended as a substitute for seeking professional guidance.

Acknowledgements

> Mother creator and cradle of dreams;
> the sustainable one in her children's storms.
>
> -Reverend Jacquelyn Jackson

To my co-authors, this book would not have come to fruition without you. I appreciate your willingness to be transparent. Thank you for your time and efforts. Thank you for sharing your journey with the world. I enjoyed our time together, those precious personal moments we've all shared to do the work. We all dug deep and pulled up precisely what we needed for cleansing, releasing, and healing. You are a brave, beautiful women with so much more in store; I can't wait to see where you go from here.

I thank God for my husband, Dave, the best cheerleader, and armor bearer a woman could find. You continue to push me and give me what I need to see my visions through. You are the epitome of a good spouse- strong, loving, kind, and corrective when I need pulling in. While writing this book, you have stood by me every step of the way. Thank you.

I am also grateful for the opportunity to be a mother. Without the experience of motherhood, I could not connect with the co-authors of this book. To Briana, Courtney, and Jonathan, I thank you for every beautiful, loving, funny, challenging, gut-wrenching, and laughable moment we have created together. You all and my grandson Xavier are the suns in my soul.

I thank God for my mother and grandmother. Their love allowed me to experience the purity of Christ in the flesh- a warmth and unconditional presence where I could be me. Their discipline gave me focus and helped me set boundaries. The fun times with them helped me to see a brighter day and future in a world that is not always inviting, friendly, or light. I know you have held my hand throughout this journey. I continue to hold you in my heart and spirit on this side until we meet again.

I thank God for my auntie, who always has my back. My first rescuer- I will never forget. You had me then as a child and you have me now. Throughout this journey you continued to tell me, I could do it, no matter what.

I have a grateful heart for my family-in-love. (The Sterling's) You all are the best! The most supportive family a woman and entrepreneur could have.

Thank you, Ms. Catherine Togba Woyee, Founder and CEO of Black Parent Magazine, for the masterfully written foreword. Your words of encouragement have been invaluable, and your excitement for the Moms' Truth is enormous. Additionally, I thank you for sharing your brilliance in the digital space, providing all things "black/brown" for every aspect of our culture.

My deep appreciation to Josiah Abraham for the book cover, marketing graphics, banners, changes, and more changes. Thank you for your patience, humility, and excellent skill. I am indebted to you for the one million reminders and for throwing in things I didn't know I needed.

Thank you to Hanah and her team at Sterling Virtual Assistant Agency for your impeccable Project Management. You are incredible!

To my village - Colette, and Jackie thank you to each of you for being a sounding board and a safe space. Your friendship is never taken lightly. To Dawn, thank you for the last minute English reminders. Terry and Loretta thank you two for always holding us in your heart, prayers and for your words of encouragement.

To Dr. Uchenna Umeh, AKA Dr. Lulu, thank you for always sharing great secrets to help another. I will never forget your guidance throughout this process. I appreciate you and the fire you bring.

Lastly, I would be remiss if I did not thank my coach and mentor, Alandria Lloyd, at The Agency by Alandria Elle, who is steadfast in her call to help others achieve greatness. Thank you for your direction and prayers.

To the reader, I hope you open the pages of this book and see yourself as the great, capable, loving mom you are. You've got this!

All my best,
Patrice Sterling

Foreword

The Moms' Truth is a must-read book from the perspective of black motherhood. The chapters in this book will introduce you to the highs and lows of black/brown motherhood; from the journey of raising black men; single parenting; parents of queer children; productive parenting; mental health challenges while parenting; advocating for them to save me; and mothering while motherless.

Because our lives are so often framed in a "culture of suffering" narrative, we must learn to give ourselves grace from fear that we have internalized the problem and made ourselves the cause, when the truth is we are oftentimes overlooked and disregarded for the compassionate, resilient, whimsical, and impassioned beings we are!

It's been 26 years since I became a mother, and in truth, it's the most challenging yet beautiful role I have ever had. Each day, and each stage, comes with a new lesson. Three lessons that have resonated with me: Motherhood is an ever-evolving process. It's important that we are willing to learn, ask for help, and accept and support our children the best way we can. Motherhood is a role, but certainly one that can be your identity is different and doesn't have to necessarily match your child's identity. No amount of parenting books, research, or advice will prepare you for motherhood.

Once you become a mother, you start to appreciate the little things much more; silence, self-care, compassionate friends, a clean space, and delicious meals. Selfcare and motherhood go hand in hand. Take care of yourself and pour into yourself so that you can benefit from the next version of you. If at any point you feel yourself slipping into depression, anxiety, shopping too much, binge eating, or being extremely exhausted, there is no shame in asking for help. You are mothering another human being, but before you're a mother, you are an individual.

As an African girl, I was always told blackberries were sweet and the blacker the berry, the sweeter the juice. I was told black coffee was strong and some people couldn't handle it. I was told my beautiful dark skin was protective and allowed me to stand in the radiant reflection of the sun. This affirmation allows me to own my place in the sisterhood of mothering as a Black woman.

Motherhood is more enjoyable to me when I take frequent breaks. Going on a date, hanging with friends, doing something solo, even aside from the breaks, I have to be doing something fulfilling for myself (woodworking, going on walks, reading, etc). And not while the kids are vying for my attention; that will be too much. As a black mother, I am concerned about issues that other mothers are not. I also have an unrivaled strength. As the mother of a black son, I must be extra vigilant in ensuring that he understands that his presence can make people feel threatened, while also assisting him in understanding his worth. As the mother of a black daughter, I am vigilant that she knows her worth, and she is never too much for a world that might not always understand her presence.

Motherhood doesn't have to be enjoyable each day. Hell, nothing is. We don't enjoy ourselves every day, let alone a child who barely knows how to be human. It's not always ideal, not always fun, but what can be, is your underlying intention of being a mother. Always do your best, always want what's best. Because let's be honest, we don't enjoy being ourselves every moment, but we do love ourselves as much as we love our kids. It's so liberating when you accept your motherhood journey as your own. You don't need to be a Pinterest mom who has her days lined up with hands-on activities and sensory play. You don't need to have a set nap schedule if it doesn't work for your little one. You can pop frozen meals in the oven and frozen breakfasts in the microwave if that's how you roll. You can have unlimited screen time and unstructured playtime. Embrace your motherhood journey.

I'm choosing to revel in the joy and pride of carrying, birthing, and raising my children in community with lots of other black mothers who love and care for them, too. Black motherhood is beautiful! We know it, and we won't stop talking about it until everyone else knows it, too.

Catherine Togba Woyee is the founder and CEO of Black Parent Magazine, Inc. Black Parent Magazine is an AI-powered digital media company that provides the most shareable breaking news, original reporting, entertainment, and video across the social web to its global audience of more than 3.9 million parents of black children.

Dedication

This book is dedicated to all the moms who wonder each day if they are getting it right. You are! To the moms who work outside the home, stay-at-home, or work-from-home, we see you, acknowledge you, and thank you. Keep up the good work—you're making a difference.

Contents

Acknowledgements i

Foreword v

Dedication ix

The Rainbow After the Storm 1
   Briana Dixon

Mission Motherhood, Joy comes in the Mourning 9
   Brianne Epps

Let Go & Let God: Imperfection, IVF & My Journey to
Motherhood 19
   Deana Spencer

Stop Acting Like a Girl! 27
   Dr. Lulu

My Moments of Weakness Made My Success 33
   Hanah Rayner

This Wasn't My Birth Plan 43
   Jazzman Brown

Her Life. Not Mine. Love is? 49
   Jennifer Brown Thompson

Supermoms have Permission to Hurt and Heal 55
  Kawanya LaTrice

If it Weren't for Them, I Wouldn't Be Productive 63
  Marie Gilder

A Mother's Silent Cry 71
  Melissa Cannon

Mothering While Motherless 79
  Nikeya Young

Advocating for them to Save Me........................ 87
  Patrice Sterling

There Is Honey in the Hard Places...................... 95
  Sonya Beavers

Why do I do what I do 103
  Stephanie Smith

It Isn't About You Anymore, Girl!..................... 111
  Takeallah Rivera

My Mom Truth.. 119
  Tosin Ola

Chapter One

THE RAINBOW AFTER THE STORM

BRIANA DIXON

My journey to motherhood started on November 17, 2016, when my OB/GYN came into the exam room whispering, "Congratulations...." I had taken a positive home pregnancy test the day before, so I made an appointment to confirm the results. At that moment, I immediately started sobbing, crying from fear, nervousness, anxiety, and joy. Being a wife and a mother had been the only consistent dream I had for myself my entire life, so the reality of being an unwed mother hit me like a ton of bricks. In addition to my own crippling fear taking over my thoughts, I had NO CLUE what my parents would think. Granted, I was twenty-nine years old at the time, they had no clue I was seeing someone, and I was living with them, so that meant my baby would be as well.

Though I was uncertain of the future, I knew I would love my baby and do the best I could to raise it. I immediately started praying over it, singing to it, talking to it, and trying to surround it with as much love as possible. Little did I know that portion of my journey would come to a screeching halt nine weeks later. At 15 weeks and three days, my water broke, and I was going into labor. I was at home alone in a panic and terrified. I called my mom repeatedly with no answer; next, I called my child's father and also got no answer. I then realized I hadn't called 911, so that was my next call. The operator was friendly and did an amazing job at keeping me calm. When the ambulance arrived, my mucus plug was on the floor in a puddle of clear and red liquids. The two days prior, I was having some discomfort/cramping, but my doctor had previously advised me that cramping was a possibility as my body changed with each new phase in my pregnancy, so I didn't think it was a big deal.

Unfortunately, the hospital closest to me did not have a labor and delivery unit, so I had to be transported to another location about 20 minutes away. The ride ended up being 30 minutes due to the rain. Amid all the chaos, I reached my God mother, who took responsibility for getting in touch with my mother. Having a village is just as important during the pregnancy as it is afterward. Once I arrived at the emergency room, I was given an ultrasound to check my fetus's heartbeat, but, in the moments before, I was being given Fentanyl to relieve the pain; it also provided a cushion as I received the devasting news. One by one, family members arrived to comfort and support me during this time. Love is so important and so greatly needed during the storm. I don't know what I would have done if I had to go through it alone. Once my mom arrived, I knew everything would be fine no matter what was going on. Another doctor came in to do a second confirmation. Once that was completed, I was given the option to have a medical procedure to remove the fetus or to take a pill that would cause me to dilate... I chose the latter. Once the doctor informed me that the procedure had a slight chance of making it impossible to conceive again, choosing that pill was a no-brainer. On January 22, 2017, I gave birth to my son while I was sitting on the toilet. Talk about adding insult to injury; I already failed at my only job as his mother, and then I couldn't even deliver him normally. The guilt I felt was overwhelming. I couldn't protect my child; I delivered him on the toilet, and then, in a moment of emotional instability, I chose not to hold him after his delivery.

That would be the first of multiple bad decisions I made in my fragile emotional state. At this point, the undiagnosed depression I had been battling for years had completely taken over. It hurt to be awake, and because of dreams, it hurt to sleep, so at a certain point, I didn't want to do either. Thank God He had a different plan for me. In the following year, my mental health became virtually non-existent. As I learned to function in my grief, there was still a yearning for a second chance at motherhood. I was supposed to have a baby, but he wasn't here, so what did I do? That's right; I got pregnant again; in May 2018, I received a positive pregnancy test result. Though I had planned for this baby, it wasn't with good intentions, nor was I in my right mind. Also, I had chosen a man that was not fit to be a father. I had to make the toughest and most painful decision I had ever made in my life to end the pregnancy. Yes, that seems a bit backward and confusing, but nothing within me felt right about that pregnancy. It wasn't just the fear of history repeating itself but the clarity I received during the six-week gestational period that helped me see it was all wrong. That was the point of my mental break when I started to heal, and feeling better wasn't just a facade.

I guess that was the right decision because, on February 26, 2020, I found out I was pregnant again. I was obviously nervous, as any woman in my situation would be, but this felt destined. There was no doubt, no fear or anxiety about being this child's mother… those feelings came later. This pregnancy, however, was not the easiest on my body, but this was the rainbow God blessed me with after my storm, so I knew I couldn't give up. Being worried and nervous at the prospect of having to raise my child without his biological father weighed on me heavily, so God gave me the best co-parent anyone could ever ask for. My son's father is one of my closest friends; even though we are not in a relationship, we are a family and act as such.

Just remember, as long as you're alive, you can always try again.

BIO

Briana Dixon was born on April 22, 1987, in Oakland, Ca. Raised in a Baptist church by a loving family gave Briana a sense of faith that has carried her throughout her life. As the eldest amongst her siblings, Briana developed a love and yearning for motherhood. She brought forth an amazing, beautiful baby boy. When Briana is not busy as the best mother possible, she works as an Executive Assistant or spends time with her family.

She also enjoys attending concerts (singing along to every word) with her friends and enjoying life.

To reach her, visit her Instagram page: @authorbrianadixon.

Chapter Two

Mission Motherhood, Joy comes in the Mourning

Brianne Epps

I have observed something else under the sun. The fastest runner doesn't always win the race, and the strongest warrior doesn't always win the battle. The wise sometimes go hungry, and the skillful are not necessarily wealthy. And those who are educated don't always lead successful lives. It is all decided by chance, by being in the right place at the right time. Ecclesiastes 9:11 NLT. When you receive the news that you are about to become a mother, something in the atmosphere shifts. The journey of the life you once knew as just being a woman elevates into a divine mission to nurture, love, and protect a blessing God handpicked especially for you. From the moment they're placed into your arms until the day God declares Mission Accomplished, they'll be many trials and tribulations. One thing I know for certain from and through experience is that trouble doesn't always last and if you happen to be in mourning, joy, and I do mean Unspeakable Joy is on the other side of it.

Now let me tell you my mission in motherhood began way before I became a mother. At the tender age of ten years old, my now late mother, Virginia L. Epps, transitioned one year after her mother, my maternal grandmother. My mother is and will always be my latest and greatest inspiration—a true woman of faith.

She loved people with her whole heart. She gave her time, resources, wisdom, and love to masses of people genuinely with no strings attached. I can remember every random act of care she did without recognition or obligation. Her poetry and short stories were so beautifully worded they pierced the depths of your heart and soul while reading. She made sure I participated actively in school and church. The foundation of faith, family, and love would carry me until I later had children. I know that God used her for the ten years she was with me to stir up my gifts spiritually and naturally. My grandmother was a Chef, tried and true. She loved her food, children, and husband as she did God Himself. I learned how to praise God, clap my hands, cook cornbread, and get my children and man together, all while gleaning from her standing up in a kitchen chair. One month after my mother passed, her father passed while babysitting my younger brother, cousin, and me. My grandfather was a deacon and what we would call a jack of all trades, which stood in the gap for my father, who was so loving and fun in his season of fathering but was also troubled battling mental health and addiction himself. I instantly picked up the weight of mourning in addition to adjusting to becoming what I know now to be a village-raced child. Nothing was easy about it. I was a child that grew into an adult and motherhood longing for my mother, and she was never coming back. My father was incarcerated for most of my childhood, so our relationship was estranged. Longing for them turned into a web of depression, rebellion, promiscuity, and unhealthy coping mechanisms of marijuana and alcohol. I will forever be indebted to my eldest aunt Joyce who selflessly went from aunt to bonus mom in the course of a year, taking on everything that came with my brother and me and already being a full-time mom to her only son.

Even though God's grace is and will always be sufficient, I still had to endure the hardships attached to my rebellion. I was lost, confused, hurt, and still very burdened by the loss of my mother when I met the man who felt like my place of escape from my dysfunctional life as I knew it. At nineteen years old, a trip to the ER for what I thought was the flu turned into getting the news that I was pregnant. At that very moment, I knew my life was about to change forever. And it definitely did, and can I tell you it got worse before it got better. Running from one type of dysfunction, I created a ten times worse dysfunctional situation. What I ran to for escape turned into a spiraling storm of a relationship full of mental, physical, and emotional abuse. In between all our partying, fighting, breaking up, and making up, we welcomed three beautiful children, two daughters and one son. Six months after our second daughter was born, I found out I was six weeks pregnant, and I made one of the most horrible decisions I've ever made to abort the child by taking what I thought was the easy route. I requested the pill process instead of surgery, so I endured going through full labor while working as a waitress for Waffle House. My manager noticed my discomfort and allowed me to go home, where I would later flush my lifeless seven-week developed child down the toilet. November 15, 2015 is a day that changed me drastically, and five months later, in April, I found out I was pregnant with my eldest son. At 24, I was now a mother with three children out of wedlock, grieving a child I didn't give a chance under the circumstance and with no goals accomplished. I had allowed my escape route and everything attached to my birthing season to drive me to what seemed to be a bottomless pit. I was ashamed and hurt; my children were the only light in this place. I suffered anxiety and depression in deep silence before my children, but we know everything that dwells in the dark must come to light. Between losing more family members and friends, not having proper childcare, losing hope in completing school after having more children, not being able to work and sufficiently provide, and finally coming to the realization that a man I loved more than myself was not who God had for me. I was now a ticking time bomb. So once the postpartum depression began to show, Psychosis surfaced. Yes, my mental health was shattered in pieces to what was almost the point of no return. I was hospitalized on three different occasions between two facilities and was diagnosed with something new and, above all, things contrary to who I knew God had called me to be each time. After the third hospitalization, I began to take my mental health seriously. I was finally free enough from guilt and shame to open up to and receive the help and healing process I always needed. For a while, things were going great; I had a regimen for my mental health, a stable income working a job I loved, dependable transportation, and I was even open to love again. And then life began to happen again. We all know that tests and trials come simply to test our faith in God. But in this process, I learned I was still weak, and everything God had helped me build up in pride, silence, and shame again I allowed to be torn down. Yet still motivated in tribulation, I attempted to build my life back, but mentally and emotionally, I was still not ready. Now in a backslidden state, I conceived my last-born son. Everything I was praying for was coming in the form of reverse! When I asked God to let my next birth be my business. I conceived a child that, under the circumstances, was putting everybody in every part of my business except the one paying me. As if that wasn't enough, the pay I petitioned God for, I mean, every zero I added to my salary while writing my vision and making it plain, was now being presented to me on a Paternity test. This man that I had lived out a whole movie script with for 15 months was not my son's father. The reality of "mama's baby, daddy's maybe" was now added to my resume. It's always been my nature to attempt to align my shortcomings, even in shame, so I decided to allow my son to build a relationship with his real father. He is a former coworker I met while working my first job as a line server after I had my first daughter. Ironically our son was a product of our long time no see conversation we had while I was seeking work at this place again. Later on, I would walk in rage, chaos, and deep regret because if I had taken the time to talk a little longer, I would've known that this man had an estranged wife, psychotic mistresses, and a back pocket full of lies that would make you question your truth. Now with all these in mind, I know you are thinking, she snapped again. A woman who was growing and labeling herself a woman of God in a repetitive cycle of depression and deceit. That's something that had to break and finally did. God began the process to my promise! I gave everything to God and took my life back. He began the stretching, the rebuke, the molding, and with tears in my eyes, I, one by one, began to release every chain, weight, false identity, and expectation. He strategically ordered my steps to my true identity in Him and my mission of Motherhood. I was born to be an overcomer, to glow from the very things that were assigned to keep me at a low and fruitless state. In building myself and this new special relationship with God, doors that I never thought I would step foot through opened. Above all things, I gained access to finally experience Joy unspeakable, Joy in my Mourning of the four beautiful angels God handpicked especially for me. He covered my womb four times to send me the ones who would cover me with everything vital to heal every wound to come with the storms of mothering them village inspired yet still motherless. Their conversations, laughs, and love would aid me enough in seeking and obtaining more than I ever imagined I could. Each one of their smiles and whit helped build my confidence. My home was sustained in and out of seasons of lack. The greatest blessings I have received wouldn't have been released if my children did not exist. So, to the mother who will stumble across my story and any of this you can relate to, let me say this, "When it comes to your mental health, Girl, deal with it before it deals with you!" If you are a woman of faith, remember and stand firm on the promises of God concerning you! When you are weak, build yourself up with the word, the bible. Ma'am, backsliding to the bottle brings babies with bottles! Love yourself and your children enough to seek and receive the help you need to truly be who you were called to be. It's okay to go to God and therapy too. Reference Romans 8:28 and Philippians 4:13. This is my personal strength and life in scripture daily. When my mission is finally accomplished in motherhood, there will be Joy unspeakable, Joy in the Mourning.

BIO

Brianne' Epps is a woman of faith, mother of four beautiful children, author, and Chef. She resides in Jackson, MS where she advocates the success and self-sufficiency of single mothers and fathers in faith, finance, and mental health. She is also currently President of the Unstoppable Divas of Mississippi's Chapter of Thicknation, a national plus size organization of women and men working hard to make a difference in their communities through service, love, and resource. Brianne' has always had a heart for people and enjoys encouraging and feeding everyone she meets. By age 25, she had reached many in her community through encouraging words and hearty meals.

Brianne' also has a small home-based catering business that she's currently transitioning into to a food truck and building a nonprofit organization. Acquired Taste LLC., Mothers on the Move and Fathers out Front Incorporated. When she's not working, she loves to write poetry/short stories, leisure time by the water for relaxation and inspiration, and spending intimate time with her children. As purpose driven as she is she humbly walks daily in her Pit to Palace experience. She strives to make Jesus famous again for his divine healing power and ability to make those who were last at the anointed and appointed time first.

Chapter Three

Let Go & Let God: Imperfection, IVF & My Journey to Motherhood

Deana Spencer

Imperfection, IVF & My Journey to Motherhood is my personal story of becoming a mother, the stigma of IVF, the love, hope, tears, and imperfections. This chapter will also provide a peek into my own discovery of "my mother's gift" to me that would unknowingly prepare me for my journey to motherhood. Today, God has blessed me with two beautiful, smart, funny, black sons. Welcome to my truth. It's my journey to motherhood in courage and faith. It's my goal to bring awareness to the possibilities of motherhood.

My Mother's Gift

After starting this project, many of my forgotten childhood memories began to resurface. The good, bad and beautiful. My mother, Sarah Geraldine Long, was born in Chicago in 1947. She was the baby of fifteen children (seven miscarriages prior) and took pride in being the baby.

There are three siblings alive today. My mother gave birth to two children, my older brother Eric (deceased) and I was born in 1973, yes, a 70s baby, the best era, I might add. The road was rough and was not easy for my mother on her own journey to motherhood. We were taught life lessons through her "small talks" or readings and poems. I had no idea they would carry me throughout life and give me the courage in my own quest to conceive. In many cases, as a child, I had no idea what she was teaching, but as I became older, I surely became wiser and understood the lessons, especially the lessons on mothering.

Imperfections

In 1991, I would meet my partner and now husband years later. During our courtship - do they call it that today? We talked about what kind of parents we would become and had conversations about what kind of parents we wouldn't become. Little did I know my "imperfections" would soon creep in years later after trying to conceive. You see, I had not really connected the dots of my maternal history, bite-size conversations about infertility and miscarriages. No one talked about how this could possibly be my story when I decided to become a mother. No one really even talked about trying to conceive before thirty or forty years of age. I was unaware that women didn't have an unlimited number of "healthy" eggs, that women had other fertility options, or if adoption was the best fit. This wasn't the type of thing discussed at the kitchen table of many black women I knew or even at many of my all-female social gatherings. You see, I tried to conceive in my 30s, and it was not easy.

I was told by doctors that I waited too late, I don't have enough "good" eggs, have my partner get checked out, or maybe motherhood is just not in the cards for you. I started to think I was flawed or cursed by God or even my maternal history and the issues my mother and grandmother had when they tried to conceive. I never wanted to go through what my mother went through with her pregnancies, including tubal pregnancies and several miscarriages.

Remember, my grandmother had seven of her own.

Well, it started to happen to me at thirty, and while time passed, my doubt, self-talk, and guilt crept in, leaving me to feel like I had failed myself, my husband, and my mother. You see, growing up was not all glam & glory. In hindsight, my mom did the best she could and parented my brother and me the best she knew how. There were definitely imperfections of my mom that I am slowly learning to heal from even at forty-nine, but I know that she loved us unconditionally and made sure we had the best education and outside activities kid could want. It was my faith, my husband, and my mother who gave me the courage not to give up.

The Journey: Let Go and Let God

For many black women, the isolation of infertility is increased with the barriers to treatment. This was my truth when I began researching my options. I first thought HELL, we can't afford this treatment. Black women don't do this to have a baby! Fifteen years ago, I started on my quest for motherhood and what I experienced was prejudice from physicians and feelings of shame and isolation. Once I sought care, I found myself feeling deeply uncomfortable in many medical spaces that were overwhelmingly white. In 2005, I finally found an African-American woman gynecologist that helped me on my journey, which included taking infertility pills. For a long time, the pills didn't seem to work, and I stopped taking them. I was angry, confused, and mad at the world. Once I gave it up to God, I got pregnant with our first son. In-between times I had a horrible early-miscarriage that resulted in surgery and scar tissue. I sought out other alternatives that would lead to my IVF process. This was probably the most emotionally draining rollercoaster I have ever been on, but eight years later, it was well worth everything we went through. We now have our second son, that completes our family.

Life's Lessons

I never knew my grandmother, but I know the stories of her trials of infertility and that of my own mother's path to conception. I have two beautiful sons who are gifts from God even when I was told that having children was impossible for me. The treatment of black women and maternal issues is an injustice that has plagued our communities for far too long. My two sons are a testimony to my faith, my willingness never to give up, and my drive to tell my story to help another woman on the path to becoming a mother.

Bio

Deana Spencer, born and raised in Chicago in the Noble Square community, is a wife and mother of 2 sons. She earned her B.A. in Visual Communications in Design from Southern Illinois University and her Masters in Early Childhood Development. Professionally, she has served as a leader in the field of early care & educational policy for over 25 years. Her passion lies in urban education, and her mission is to create family-centered programs that help prevent the intergenerational cycle that poor education presents for children and their parents. She has worked on various policy-driven initiatives throughout Illinois. She is a past Erikson Institute Early Learning Policy Fellow, who continues to help transform under-served communities in Chicago, including parenting initiatives. In her current role, she serves as the Director of Early Learning & Policy for Holy Family Ministries. She is an active member of the National Black Child Development Institute and a proud member of Alpha Kappa Alpha Sorority, Incorporated.

Chapter Four

STOP ACTING LIKE A GIRL!

Dr. Lulu

Words that I repeatedly used to "admonish" my eldest child when she was younger. How I wish I could take those words back. How I wish I never uttered any one of them. How I wish I never felt the need to say such words. How I wish I never felt the need to make her feel anything but whole. How I wish…

Last week during her final recital at the New England Conservatory of Music, she gave me many accolades. The audience gave me a special ovation, and my heart was happy, but I didn't miss it. While she praised me for supporting her music career from the jump, she didn't mention my name when it came to supporting her gender, her transition, and her true self.

She talked about her friends and classmates and named them one by one; she mentioned how their friendship and affirmations helped literally save her life. She didn't mince her words. I am very grateful for them; I only wish it had been me.

As I sit and write this, my heart is heavy and sad. It is filled with tears unshed, words unspoken, hugs ungiven, love unshared. I am filled with emotions. Why did I not affirm her when she was younger? Why was my heart closed to seeing her the way she really was? Why did I allow fear to reign and rain on me?

It has been two years since my eldest child, who was assigned male at birth, shared about her non-binary gender and they/them pronouns. It has been five months since she shared her transgender identity and her pronouns. And it has been two weeks since she shared her new name with me.

Ironically, I had picked that exact name for her in my mind. I know my child. I breastfed her for 22 months. I was there through her fevers as a newborn, scrapes and bruises, tests and exams, recitals, and awards. I knew the name I *should have* given her, and she ended up picking that name of all the names in the world!

Even though I am relieved because it is all now out in the open, I am still sad and in mourning. I am scared stiff about the unknown. She has begun transitioning, taking her Estrogen pills and Testosterone blockers. She is "finally free" to be her real self, as she said in her closing speech. I can only imagine what that must feel like.

I cannot even envision what it means to finally live free! The closest I have come to experiencing any kind of freedom was the day my divorce was final from her now ex-father. Even that is only a tiny percentage of what she must truly be experiencing. Sheer, true unadulterated freedom!

The freedom to breathe fresh air, the freedom to live life in your own skin, the freedom to just be who you are... a concept that so many of us take for granted: A freedom to exist and take up space.

The other day on the phone, she described our home as *very transphobic* when she was a child. All I could do was listen in regret. I could barely say the words "I am sorry" without choking up. I wish I had never played a role in any of that, but I did.

And that is why with tears rolling down my cheeks as I write this, I implore you, dear mom or dad or parent, to read these words with an open heart, "Accept your child."

You are a vessel to bring your child into this earth. You are their first love, and they are an extension of your heart. Loving them is a must. Understanding that they are individuals is a must. Allowing them to become who they are is a must.

Be careful not to think or plan too far ahead. Enjoy them here and now. Rethink the thoughts you allow in your head, the words you say out of your mouth, and the way you act and treat them in your home. You are and will remain the most influential person in their lives, and that is a fact.

Ultimately, we must decide if we want to continue being in our children's lives or if we do not. Because they will grow up and become who they were meant to be. Or we could inadvertently drive them to jump (to their deaths) while trying to please us. It is a tough pill, but we must swallow it.

Several days ago, I sent her a text message telling her just how proud I am of her and her insistence on living her truth regardless of anyone else's thoughts. I ended the text with, "I just want you to know that I have always wanted a daughter."

I waited a few minutes for a response, and just as I decided she would probably ignore it, I felt the buzz of the vibration indicating a response text, and it read. "Mom, you have always had a daughter."

Bio

Dr. Lulu aka the Momatrician is a Nigerian-born, pediatrician and mom of three including a non-binary transgender adult. She is a life coach, TEDx speaker, bestselling author of 5 books, LGBTQ* advocate, and youth suicide prevention activist.

A former Lt. Col and commander in the US Air Force and disabled veteran, she is currently working with parents of LGBTQ+ kids. She is also a teen confidence coach.

Dr. Lulu speaks publicly on parenting, childhood trauma, LGBTQ issues, women issues, entrepreneurship, and suicide prevention. She has been featured on local, national, and international television including the nationally syndicated CBS This Morning with Gayle King. She lives and works in San Antonio, Texas.

Chapter Five

My Moments of Weakness Made My Success

Hanah Rayner

Don't let your moments of weakness define you as a person.

I met my partner at just sixteen years old. It's interesting because it's rare to meet your one true love so young these days. I just knew he was the one from the second I saw him. It's safe to say that many friends and family doubted our relationship because of our youth. Over the years, like any couple, we've been through our ups and downs.

At just eighteen years old, we experienced our first miscarriage together. It wasn't something we ever talked about. We both dealt with it in very different ways. I'd find myself eating my weight in chocolate every night, and he would fill any spare pockets of time that he had. To mask the feelings of loss, we bought a puppy, Louie. From that point onwards, our relationship moved quickly. One year later, we decided to move out into a rented property, and a year after that, at just twenty years old, we bought our first house.

For two years after my miscarriage, we were trying for a baby. At twenty-one, after two years of crying every month, when my period came, which was often delayed by stress, I finally fell pregnant.

I had a stable job as a secretary at one of Europe's top patent firms, and we earned good money between us both. We had our own home and a family dog; the moment couldn't have been more perfect. There's so much pressure on young women to strive for perfection. There was an expectation of being happy and enjoying pregnancy because, on paper, I had everything I could have asked for. In all honesty, being pregnant was one of the hardest periods of my life.

As soon as I fell pregnant, people were quick to judge. They commented on how fast I fell pregnant, whether I'd be a stay-at-home mother, and if I could even afford to have a child or return to work. Quickly after getting pregnant, I became quite ill and found myself staying in hospital overnight every other week for weeks at a time. My parents were four hours away and rarely came to visit because of the distance; my partner worked long hours, and I'd never felt more alone. As soon as he closed the front door to leave for work, I'd break down crying, and negative thoughts would creep in. The truth is, despite desperately wanting to expand our family, I couldn't have been unhappier.

At sixteen weeks, I was taken to hospital to see a psychiatrist as I've had suicidal thoughts. I felt like I was in a constant battle with my mind. Little did I know, my placenta started maturing at thirty-four weeks, and I went into the hospital to be induced at thirty-six weeks. It was the start of the first lockdown, labour was difficult, and I was in the hospital on my own for most of it.

My birthing experience was traumatic, to say the least. I lost a lot of blood, and my partner had to leave two hours after active labour. I was all alone again. I passed out and woke up in intensive care. No one could visit, I didn't want to share the news with anyone, and I didn't want to talk to anyone.

The first few weeks after giving birth, things were okay. Then my partner went back to work, and I was all alone again. It was just me and baby, the lockdowns, and my thoughts. Everyone would encourage me to enjoy this stage, but I felt like my "normal" life had been taken away from me. I dreaded meeting friends and family. They'd talk to me about my daughter's feeding times or toileting schedule. I wasn't interested in sharing all the details. I felt like the odd person in a room of six.

Months passed until the day I decided I needed to take action. I didn't want to be a stay-at-home mum. I wanted to create a life for myself. I had youth on my side and was ready to make a change and a decision that would change my life. I decided to start my own business in the middle of a pandemic with my baby.

Starting a business isn't a job - it's a lifestyle choice. It gave me a purpose, adventure, and, most importantly, something to think about. Instead of going to baby groups and making mum friends, I worked hard to find clients and create a personal brand.

By Christmas, the depression started to lift, and I began to learn a new thought process: healing. The guilt that I felt for feeling the way I did was intense. But, with time, I worked through these feelings. As humans, we're stronger than we might think. With inner mindset work, we learn that anything is possible. During this period, I fell pregnant again. I was at high risk and lost the baby at just six weeks. I made time for myself for the first time in a long time.

Feeling more motivated than ever, despite the sleepless nights, I found that the key to moving forward was finding the balance between work, family time, and rest.

Coming up to two years, I am now an empowered CEO of my agency and have a growing team. I spend as much time as possible with my partner and daughter, and I've never been happier.

I'm only twenty-three and still have so much growing to do, but I'm ready for the next stage of my life with my partner, my toddler, Louie, and my agency. I've reached my version of success.

Now, I focus on my goals and not on the words of others around me.

My word of advice - Keep your expectations high on your goals and low on people.

Bio

Hanah is 23 years old, born in England but is also half Mauritian. She is a fiancée, a loving mother and an agency owner.

She runs Sterling Virtual Assistant Services and offers business and marketing support and also offers coaching sessions to new virtual assistants.

She is a certified Executive PA and CILEx qualified Legal Secretary, with a combined sales and secretarial background.

Her goals are to continue growing her business, whilst spending more time with her family.

She loves reading and watching her daughter learn new things. Her favourite thing to do is explore on family holidays and long dog walks.

Chapter Six

This Wasn't My Birth Plan

Jazzman Brown

When I was twenty-three years old, a pregnant friend and I were having lunch. While we were eating, she mentioned the term "Birth Plan." I had never heard the term before and asked  her to explain. She stated it's a detailed plan on how you want to bring your baby into the world. Later that day, I went home and planned my "birth plan. "To be clear, I was not in a relationship or pregnant. However, I'm a planner, so I planned. I decided on a water birth at Kaiser in Walnut Creek, where I could attempt natural birth, but if the pain was too real, I could renege. My mom and husband, whomever he was going to be, would be in the room when it was time to push. It was a perfect plan for entering motherhood.

You know the saying, "Wanna make God laugh, tell Him your plans?" Well, I made God roll on the floor laughing. At twenty-seven, I married a tall drink of water named Deonte, aka Tay.

Let's just say we did a lot of practicing trying to get the "baby show" on the road. However, I wasn't really in a rush because I wanted the first two years of marriage without kids, but if it happened, I wouldn't be mad; I had my birth plan ready.

Soon after I turned twenty-eight, a friend of Tay asked if we could keep her two daughters, ages three and five, so she could work on herself. She said she would help with childcare and drop off food weekly since she gets government assistance. Also, during tax time, she would give some money for clothes. She would still be responsible for them; we were just supporting her in this time of need. We were already watching the girls Friday-Sunday; what's four more days a week, I thought. Plus, she will still be active and help financially. We can all be one big happy family. Did you notice I had yet another plan on how this would turn out?

We obtained legal guardianship to enroll them in my health benefits. At the time, the oldest had a major anxiety disorder, while the youngest had attachment issues with adverse reactions to transitions. She would have extreme tantrums. Also, she would not go to sleep unless I rocked her to sleep EVERY night.

We had weekly visits with their biological mother (bio-mom); most were going to plan. Except we were not getting any of the financial help promised for the kids. We didn't press the issue because our family came together and chipped in to help us. However, childcare was $1200 per kid a month out of pocket. That was a lot for us and would not be sustainable.

Contact with the bio-mom started to dwindle, then completely stopped about eight months into the arrangement. NOTHING was going as planned. "Mayday Houston… We have several problems!" My credit cards were maxed out. Help from our village was great but not enough for the need. My plan had failed, epically.

After reaching out to several agencies and nonprofits for help, we got connected to a group called KinShip. They showed us free resources that helped us a lot. "Amen, the crisis was over!" Echoed in my head. Now I just need to deal with the toddler's behavioral issues. Bi-weekly therapy appointments became the norm. I didn't mind because the girls were making a complete 360. Their therapist Dr. April was a God send. I thought life was starting to get back on the road to my plan. Yeah... No, I was really wrong. Little did I know that was just the beginning of a hellish battle.

The KinShip we received was funded through the state. When we were approved, it referenced the kid's information and detected the kids were still enrolled in other programs under their bio-mom. Our approval stopped all her financial benefits. She was outraged and immediately asked for the kids' back.

As much as this wasn't my plan to keep the girls longer than a year, I had to deny her request. I inquired about the steps she needed to take to be a better mother, i.e., therapy, saving money, and keeping in contact with the kids. Sadly, she hadn't done any of them. This series of events would land us in and out of court for the next three years. This was the most stressful period of my life.

I was called everything but a child of God. I was belittled in court as the woman who stole her kids. She even tried to fight me in front of the courthouse. As strange as it sounds, her words really made me second guess myself. I had no clue if I was doing a good job. I was just fighting with everything I had to keep the girls safe and loved.

Around the third year, I had gone from emotional in court to cold. Nothing she said bothered me. After an encounter in court, their bio mom said something that somehow made it through my cold demeanor. She stated, "You stole my kids because you can't have your own." It hit me like a ton of bricks. It had been three years, and I was way off my plan's timeline. My son should have been about one at this point.

I instantly made a doctor's appointment after that interaction. After a month of testing, Tay and I sat in a fertility doctor's office, where my worst fear was confirmed.

I was told my right fallopian tube had scar tissue from an STD I had once upon a time. The scar tissue allowed my fallopian tube to dilate, making it nearly impossible to conceive naturally. A stupid decision to have premarital sex had canceled my birthing plan. I was embarrassed, regretful, sad, and scared. "I may not ever be a mother" is all I repeated. After crying for the first 20 minutes of our ride home, Tay said, "I know this wasn't your plan, but we'll be ok. Our two girls are more than enough, and you don't have to give birth to be a mother." At that very moment, I stopped crying. He was right. I am a mother of two.

It's been a few years now since that day, and my daughters are now ten and eight. I believe God will restore my body so I can use my birth plan one day. But either way, I'm still a mother by God's great design. And that's my mother's truth.

Advice to all mothers, "Your journey may not go according to your plan, but it's going according to God's plan; so, relax and enjoy the ride because He's the best driver."

Bio

Jazzman Brown is an avid recruiter for the Kingdom of God. She is a full-time wife and mother of two feisty little girls who keep her busy and on her toes. In her free time, when Jazzman is not "mom-ing," she sings on the Praise and Worship team at the Rock Church Bay Area. She spends time with her huge family; or works in the community with her sorority, Zeta Phi Beta Inc.

Jazzman currently works as a Risk Manager for a public agency. She has a Master of Science in Human Resource Management and is certified as a Risk Manager Practitioner.

If you haven't had the pleasure of meeting this vibrant and intelligent young woman, get ready. You may learn a random fact, talk about fashion, hear a song, receive a compliment, hug, or possibly all five.

Chapter Seven

HER LIFE. NOT MINE. LOVE IS?

JENNIFER BROWN THOMPSON

Hi Babygirl! I miss you so much. What's up? Wish you were here! Mama, can you listen to me? Can we talk? Of course, Babygirl, what's up? It sounds like you have company, mama. Can you go somewhere quiet? Ok, sweetie pie – I'm listening. What came next wasn't anything I was prepared for or what I thought would be coming from my only daughter.

Before I say anything, I don't want you to make this about the kind of mother you think you are – you are a very good mother, and I'm glad you're mine and Evan's. Mama, I'm dating a woman. I literally began overthinking as I usually do... "What did I do wrong?" Is this because of the divorce? She's stressed out because we weren't able to pay for her college tuition! She should come home, I'll ask her to just come home, and I can fix it, "I'm not a good mother; this is all my fault! Mama! Can you hear me? "Yes, Babygirl, I'm just thinking..." I knew it! You are overthinking again and making this about you! Mama, this is about me, and you are a wonderful mother! Maybe I should call you back later... this is too much for you right now! No, sweetheart, I'm hearing, and I'm listening.

My daughter just shared with me that she likes women, and she's Queer. When I hear the word Queer, I think strange, weird, different, not normal... Mama, if you have questions, please ask me but don't just get quiet. I just kept asking myself, how could I have missed this? Have I been too caught up in my life and challenges that I totally didn't pay her enough attention? Clearly, I hadn't been paying her enough attention, and maybe if she were living with me, I would have seen this coming. None of this was true, and my daughter helped me realize this - We spent the next several weeks and months talking and listening to each other, and I discovered that I had a lot of misconceptions about the LGBTQ+ community.

We raised our children in a Christian home, attending church every Sunday, including Sunday School., youth choir, young adult choir…Their father is a minister, and he and other ministers preached about men and women coming together to reproduce and be married – not same-sex couples; I mean, how can two women or two men have children? I worked with our youth – so how in the world did I miss that my child was Queer? She was a cheerleader, attended a catholic high school, and went to Jr and Sr. Proms with young men – I was totally lost. Over the next several months, I listened to my daughter talk about how nervous she was to come out to her friends and family, especially me because she knew that I had plans for "Her Life," and nothing included a same-sex relationship. Her brother told her not to worry about others and what they potentially would say. He told her that if anyone said anything less than supportive of her, we would dismiss them from our lives. I agreed – this was my Babygirl that I birthed and spent 23 hours in active hard labor, and I dare anyone to make her feel anything other than amazing.

I Love you, Mama – I'm your daughter, and my love for women doesn't change that in any way. I traveled to an event where my daughter showcased some of her art and other creatives, and the woman she was dating was there. I tried to be "cool" and engage in small talk… my daughter said I was trying too hard and to just let it flow naturally. A couple of years have passed, and I now spend Mother's Day with my daughter, her girlfriend, and her family. It warms my heart to see how happy she is and how welcoming her girlfriend's family is to me, my son, and my daughter.

As a mother, my main concern is that my children are happy, have good friends, and are good friends with others. I'm learning to listen more and to trust the process because the fact is, if she were in a heterosexual relationship, I'd want the same thing for her, love, acceptance, peace, and success.

Motherhood has changed my life. Motherhood has taught me that my journey is mine and theirs is theirs - loving my children unconditionally is my role, and making myself available when they need me. It's so important to listen and not interject our opinion – we can guide them and share advice if they want to receive it, and because they may have a different opinion than ours, we can still share nuggets of wisdom with them – One day may receive it – or not 😊

Bio

Jennifer Elayne Brown Thompson - Jennifer is the Director of Human Resources and Administration for PolicyLink, a national research and action institute advancing racial and economic equity by Lifting Up What Works®.

She began her career in non-profit HR 15 years ago. Jennifer enjoys recruiting and bringing the best talent into the organization while ensuring the staff has the best benefits, compensation, training, and employee morale.

Jennifer enjoys being creative, traveling, and spending time with her family and friends. Most of all, she enjoys being a mother to Elayna and Evan.

Chapter Eight

Supermoms have Permission to Hurt and Heal

Kawanya LaTrice

In today's environment, we are becoming increasingly aware of personal health's importance beyond just the physical. I have grown to learn emotional and mental health should have a well-being strategy and routine check-ups just as we do for our bodies. Growing up, my early exposure to adverse emotional situations was not met with a doctor to help me work through the inner hurt. Or any real strategies to cope with my unfamiliar feelings; therefore, I pushed them aside and moved on to what life presented next.

Being a single parent for over twenty-plus years, early in the journey, I faced a number of struggles where my emotional limitations hindered my parenting capabilities. Despite my ignorance, enduring painful circumstances early in life with limited guidance for managing them resulted in several underdeveloped emotions deep within me. This emotional immaturity, compounded with some of the frustrations of single parenting, placed such overwhelming pressure on me that I was hurting in places unseen to others. I was tired beyond the physical; it was mental and emotional exhaustion I could not articulate or communicate; it hindered me from being fully present as a parent.

Driven by the irritation of my unstable feelings of single parenting, the drastic need for new parental strategies, and my wavering mental well-being, I was guided to seek help beyond just my spiritual and inner circles. I took a huge step that is not always popular in the black community to seek the support of a therapist to put a name to what I was experiencing. In my counseling sessions, I became comfortable enough to recall encounters that triggered hurtful emotions that I buried inside. My ability to repress these hurt feelings often times prompted me to be distrusting, over-protective, and fearful when things appeared out of my control.

Choosing therapy and committing to unlearn some emotional behaviors to create realistic parenting goals and a toolbox containing new relationship techniques for my faith, fitness, family, finances, friends, and fun would serve me immensely as a single parent. Additionally, I built the courage to face what I had suppressed unknowingly for years in therapy.

Hoping to ensure others know they are not alone with unseen pain; I want to provide a look at some feelings I encountered at different phases of life and their causes. Also, I want to share two toolbox techniques developed in therapy; bible scriptures to help me coop while working on my healing and permission statements to acknowledge my feelings.

Childhood Emotional Ordeals:

Abandonment - I vividly recall the first time I felt abandoned; it was when my mom left to join a branch of the U.S Military Service when I was maybe five/six years old. I did not understand my feelings much then, but when the little girl in me needed my mother, she was no longer present without an explanation.

Disappointment – My main encounter with this emotion was when my parents separated, and my father wasn't able to process his personal hurt & pains, triggering sporadic unreliable behaviors from a once dependable, fun-loving individual. This relationship changes significantly impacted his dependability, causing my eight-year-old mind to struggle with reconciling his new behaviors into adulthood.

Rage - I was so enraged and just plain tired of the domestic abuse my aunt endured from her boyfriend until one day, in her defense, at the age of nine, I found myself involved in a physical altercation with adults.

Fear – One night while in the car driving to my first-grade school play, our car was struck by a train that failed to signal while we were crossing the tracks. The mid-night panic attacks and nightmares that proceeded would become a fear pattern for a long time.

Scripture: So be truly glad. There is wonderful joy ahead even though you must endure many trials for a little while. 1 Peter 1:6 (NLT)

Permission: I give my inner child permission to hurt and heal from emotional neglect.

Adulthood Emotional Outpour:

Disappointment & Abandonment – These feelings resurfaced after my failed long-term relationship with my ex when plans of marriage, to create a life and grow old together were overshadowed by behaviors of emotional manipulation, verbal abuse, and infidelity.

Fear – This emotion showed up at night in the form of an overloaded mind working to solve problems for three people and anxiety from mental and emotional confusion from parenting two kids in different phases of growing into themselves.

Scripture: Even youth grow tired and weary, and young men stumble and fall. Isaiah 40:30 (NIV).

Permission: I give my adult self, permission to feel pain during a season of tribulations.

Parenting While Broken:

Rage – When my ex disregarded my efforts to set parental boundaries, it left me feeling completely disrespected. During these moments, I could feel myself becoming so enraged that I hardly recognized myself.

Suppression of Emotions – As a parent dealing with two kids, I suppressed hurt and pain often. I leaned on emotional suppression as I went through years of struggling with holding it together while dealing with a semi-present parent whose lack of effort sometimes made life physically and mentally challenging.

Scripture: He gives strength to the weary and increases the power of the weak. Isaiah 40:30 (NIV)

Permission: I give the single mother in me permission to struggle with expressing vulnerability and asking for help.

Journey to Healing:

Completing therapy gave me power mentally and emotionally, not just physically, to establish parenting goals that would allow me to do my best with my available resources. This has allowed me to parent from a place of emotional and mental peace.

Scripture: For I know the plans I have for you, "declares the Lord," plans to prosper you and not to harm you, plans to give you hope and a future. Jeremiah 29:11 (NIV)

Permission: I permit myself to use new spiritual, mental, emotional, and physical tools to parent differently.

Advice: If at any point you find yourself in a place of mental or emotional parental struggles, I hope I encouraged you to give yourself permission to parent differently by stepping outside of your regular parenting toolbox for a new framework of support.

BIO

Kawanya is a mother of two beautiful young adults, ages 26 and 20, and one delightfully energetic grandchild. She has a 20+ year financial and accounting career that has carried her across various industries. With an MS degree in Accounting and a BS degree in Finance, Kawanya has held numerous titles throughout her career. These roles included Assistant Vice President of Finance & Accounting in Insurance and Director of Finance& Operations in Education.

Led by a big heart, Kawanya focuses on sharing her knowledge. She has taught Fiscal Management classes through various volunteer efforts with organizations, such as New Life Restoration Ministries and Precious Rubies Foundation.

Kawanya's passion projects center around her love for home and family, which currently include building a home decor business and developing plans to author a family cookbook.

Message Kawanya via Instagram at uniquely_kawanyaj2.

Chapter Nine

IF IT WEREN'T FOR THEM, I WOULDN'T BE PRODUCTIVE

MARIE GILDER

As a mother of four children ranging from eleven years old to one month, I go into each day thinking I have a plan on how to tackle each moment. Reality is… that's a negative. Each one of them runs the day. From whom wakes up first to who wants a hot breakfast, down to just eating a Babybel cheese. It's interesting

because I never saw myself as that mother- you know, the one who offers three different meal plans instead of one meal with everyone sitting down to eat the same thing. That said, it's a good morning if everyone eats breakfast smoothly.

Because of the different age ranges, genders, and personalities, I learned that talking, disciplining, and even playing with my children don't always look the same. The fact that my children may need four different things simultaneously can create seconds, minutes, moments, and days of great difficulty. Thus, I work in overdrive of learning my kids almost every thought, move, cry, and even catching those moments when one kid is about to right-hook the other.

While every moment is not predictable, their futures seem to be. I see my eleven-year-old as the next up-and-coming fashionista and a world-known humanitarian. I see my three-year-old hosting a Tell All toddler talk show and later becoming the world's top surgeon. I see my almost two-year-old as a professional athlete and personal trainer to those going through physical therapy and a comedian on the side. And my one-month-old will be helping his older siblings stay out of trouble while teaching the word of God to lost souls. Although this may not be accurate, it's important to understand my children well enough to meet their needs and set them up for success.

Although every day may not feel so productive, from one that was, I must remind myself that every day is. When I watch my oldest child, Jada, take on the "mothering role," I see growth and maturity. The way she cares for her siblings and becomes their teacher and friend—giving them genuine love without even trying calms my soul. And, when she comes to me with those cringy "getting older" talks, I can see the child forming into a young lady, knowing she will make good choices.

Then I come to my second child, Mavis, and I see how she never ceases to amaze me with her nurturing ways. How she feels people's hurts and pain and knows when to ask three simple words, "Are you ok?" Or when she sees the struggle of chores or carrying groceries, how she comes out of nowhere to help without being asked or told. And even how she gets that twinkle in her eyes when you bring her a new book because she's eager to learn.

Following her is my third child and first son, Travis Jr. He's already a force to be reckoned with of protection. The way he gazed into my eyes while he was an infant to let me know, "I gotcha, mommy." And when his sisters let out squeals because they see a bug, he runs to their rescue.

It's amazing to see how much he knows he's hilarious and uses that to his advantage. He has a silent charm and lights up a room with his smile.

Finally, my fourth child, Immanuel, reminds me to take my time because of his sure and calming spirit. Oh! How he's teaching me the power of patience all over again. (Got to be careful what you pray for). And the look into his kind, beautiful eyes telling me everything is ok even in the midst of chaos is always a reassuring effect of productivity.

As I grow into the mother gang, I realize the key to keeping a productive lifestyle is understanding that I am the example that dictates how my children become productive. The road to this looks different for every parent. As parents, we have many failures while raising our kids, and it is my job to keep those failures to a minimum. I've had to change my whole way of existing as an individual because of them, and I'm grateful for that. This change has led me to believe that I wouldn't be productive if it wasn't for them!

My productivity means understanding who my children are and what they require of me as a mother. It means I do when I don't want to and sacrifice when I don't have. Being productive also means I owe it to my kids not to be selfish and to remember why God granted me this amazing task of mothering. Without them, I would be lifeless because I pour my all into their beings. Living through my children is a no-brainer because they must be better than me. I expect them to make better choices so they may have better chances of any opportunities they want out of life. As a mother, I choose to raise my children honestly about my past mistakes, so they understand life's consequences. But more importantly, to always have their trust and to create accurate listening patterns.

Furthermore, I hold myself to the highest degree of productivity by ensuring my children understand and know who God is to figure out their life's purpose. So, when Jada is not happy with me telling her no, Mavis is sad because she can't have her favorite snack, Travis Jr. feels upset because he missed a very needed nap, and Immanuel is uneasy because I'm not able to give him my full attention, I can still see through the darkness. They all fill the room with smiles and fill my soul with happiness and joy. They are loving, encouraging, and respectful children. They are literally my four added heartbeats! So, at the end of each tiring day, I remind myself not to complain; instead, I tell myself… it was a productive day!

BIO

Marie Annette Gilder made her debut in the world on May 14, 1988. Marie attended schools in California, North Carolina, and Grafenwoehr, Germany. After graduating from Berkeley High in 2006, Marie decided to pursue a career in Education, working for Berkeley Unified School District. Marie's journey has allowed her to grow and develop as a mother, daughter, sister, and aunt. The love she sacrifices for her four children is unmeasurable. Devoting her life to God, Marie is one of the most courageous, determined, compassionate, loving, strong persons, you will ever meet.

Chapter Ten

A Mother's Silent Cry

Melissa Cannon

On the surface, Vanessa appears to have all her ducks in a row as she maneuvers through her daily life, raising her three children and encouraging others to be the best they can be every day during her career. Secretly she suffers in silence, pushing her faded memories to the side and focusing on life's unexpected challenges to effortlessly put her children's health, safety, and security before her own until she realizes that her own health is deteriorating. After having her final child, she received confirmation from the doctor's office. Vanessa's heart began to shatter as she heard she was diagnosed with chronic depression. During that same week, her mother passed, and she now has to care for their autistic brother, who has taken her career to a spiraling halt. With three children to raise and her brother, she is forced to make a decision to fight for her life and face the demons she kept hidden for so long or continue to live carrying the weight of her secret silence. A secret she had kept for over thirty years had finally taken a toll on her life, her body, and, as badly as she did not want to admit, her mind. Vanessa could no longer bear the suffering of yesterday's past. Vanessa decided to share her truth and be open about her experiences growing up with an abusive mother.

Vanessa grew up in a very loving, caring, and happy home. Her mama Rosie was a very well-dressed, sophisticated, and astonishingly beautiful black woman. Rosie was a stay-at-home mother of three children and loved being a mother. She was a very nurturing and disciplined woman. She was well respected everywhere she went, being very active in children's lives. Rosie was PTA president of three schools and was very influential in the community. Jackson Nessa's dad owned a construction company, worked long hours, and provided a very comfortable life for his family. Behind those walls of silver and gold, closed life appeared to be very different. At a very young age, Vannessa knew she would be punished if she did not do things exactly as her mother advised. Vanessa knew something was different about her mother's behavior, and as she got older, she realized how much.

Vanessa's parents divorced at a very young age, and Rosie moved her children to a new city. With no one to visit, Vanessa's abuse behind closed doors became normal. Vanessa transitions into adulthood and lands her dream job as a Business Development Strategist. She tells her mother the awesome news, and Rosie begins to get so infuriated that she punches Vanessa in the face and blackens her eye. Vannessa went to work the next day; she did not say anything, covering her face with tons of makeup like usual. Vanessa can no longer take the abuse and decides she will plan an exit for her and her children. She decided to research support groups to see if they shared similar experiences, and to her surprise, she was comforted to know that she was not alone. As Vanessa then plans to move away to start fresh for her children.

Country life was the best living. That was until Vanessa received a phone call from her daughter saying that Rosie pulled her hair out from her scalp because Sunny would not admit to having sex with Rosie's new boyfriend. Sunny was only nine years old. Vanessa's worst nightmare had come to pass! Thinking that her mother wouldn't harm her grandchildren and the cycle of dysfunctional chaos had ended, Vanessa rushed four hours back to check on Sunny's safety. Rosie had finally checked herself into a hospital. Vanessa was very upset with her mother, but her generational curses had trickled down to haunting her daughter. Vannessa knew it took a lot of strength for her mother to admit something was wrong.

About two weeks went by when Vanessa decided to surprise her mama with some homemade peach cobbler and her latest pregnancy announcement. Vanessa arrives home, checks the mailbox, and the neighbor says, I saw your mother the other day, and she had the same clothes as last week. Rushing into the house, she finds her mother has passed away. Falling to her knees in agony, mixed emotions immediately filled her mind as Vanessa tried to get her thoughts together. There was not enough time to grasp all the emptiness Vanessa's soul felt. It was as if there was still time. The pathologist confirmed that Rosie passed due to suicide. Several months pass and Vanessa begins to break the silence of her mother's relationship and decides to talk to a therapist. Therapy was something that Vanessa always knew she needed but continued to subconsciously allow the patterns of denial and fear to cloud her decision and kept putting it off. Vanessa never realized how much trauma was hiding. She realized that her views on life were only a perception of the experiences she faced growing up. Vanessa soon realized that her mother was abusing her grandchildren as well. Sophia and Sunny, in fact, experienced some of the same childhood abuse as Vanessa.

With help from a family therapist, Vanessa managed to regain the love and strength she needed to truly love herself and build a relationship with her three beautiful daughters Therapy helped her teach her daughters the importance of knowing how to love themselves wholeheartedly. Never give up on yourself. Motherhood isn't easy; it is one of the most rewarding gifts, but to suffer in silence does not help anyone. Finding the right doctor helped Vanessa understand that she was not alone, and the experiences she held hostage in her mind for so long were a reflection of how she was treated. It is okay to talk about it publicly. It is okay to admit that you are not okay and get the help you deserve.

Bio

Certified Personal Trainer, Melissa Cannon, has been developing custom workouts for personal training in Birmingham for five years, largely due to the immediate results from her simple exercises and lifestyle changes. Her techniques were proven when she lost 120 lbs in 15 months.

Her clients range from mothers who want to regain their natural physique to individuals striving for breakthrough results and 9-year-old kids learning to appreciate their health. With a client list as diverse as her personal training methods, she regularly works with women of extraordinary talents whose daily routines are filled with endless tasks and business executives desiring increased energy and strength.

Melissa has appeared in various fitness publications. She has created all personal workout programs, including a YouTube Channel, Stay Snatched 24/7.

She has three daughters and a brother. Although balancing family and a career may be tough sometimes, she believes that finding time for yourself and your health is very important and an excellent example for family. She has transformed thousands of lives through fitness and healthy lifestyle changes.

Education and Certifications

Stay Snatched 24/7 Fit Club Owner

Holistic Spiritual Life Coach Certification

National Academy of Sports Medicine - Certified Nutritionist

National Academy of Sports Medicine - Certified Personal Trainer

Mental Health Advocate

Domestic Abuse Advocate

Chapter Eleven

MOTHERING WHILE MOTHERLESS

Nikeya Young

On Monday, April 24, 1995, at approximately 4:00 pm, I became a motherless child. My mother succumbed to severe peritoneal infection (she had Lupus and was on Peritoneal Dialysis at the time) and passed away at just forty-six years old. I was only fourteen at the time. When you're a kid, people in their forties seem old. But at the time of this writing, I am forty-one years old, and I have a newfound appreciation for just how YOUNG you are when you are in your forties! There was no cure for Lupus, so my mother always knew that death was a possibility for her, but she prayed and had faith that God would allow her to live to see me grow up. And in a way, her prayers had been answered. My mother's first brush with severe illness and potential death occurred when I was just two years old, so God gave us twelve additional years together. The next four years after my mother's death can be best described as tumultuous and unstable. I lived in three different households with relatives between 1995 and 1999 (the year I graduated from high school). Upon graduating high school, I was accepted to DePaul University, and I moved from my hometown of Tulsa, Oklahoma, to Chicago, Illinois. I have resided in Illinois ever since.

Anyone who has lost a parent can tell you how traumatic it can be. There is never a good time to say goodbye to the people responsible for bringing you into this world. And while they say that time heals all wounds, there are still scars that remain. By the time I became a mother for the first time in 2016, I was thirty-five years old, and my mother had been gone for twenty-one years. Nevertheless, almost as soon as I discovered I was pregnant, I began to long for my mother. It's difficult to describe, but a new, fresh wave of grief began to wash over me throughout the pregnancy. I had SO MANY QUESTIONS that I wanted to ask her! She and I would joke about the day that I would grow up and get married and have children. She vowed that she would spoil them rotten (playing with them endlessly, baking for them and teaching them how to cook, etc.) And now, that moment was fast approaching... and she wasn't here. Getting through high school, college, my wedding day, and many other big milestones without her was ONE thing, but getting through motherhood without her was QUITE ANOTHER!

One of the best things that my mother did for me as a parent was to make sure that I had a firm foundation in Christ. She was a Sunday School Teacher and an avid reader of the Bible, so naturally, she weaved God into everything she did and everything she taught me. At the time of her passing, I was a newly pubescent teenager with the mood swings to match! At times I'm sure that she probably questioned whether or not ANY of her instructions were getting through to me at all. But the faith that she instilled in me from a very young age helped me overcome the grief and mental battles that I was fighting both during and after my pregnancy. I read faith-based books on childbirth and motherhood. I journaled. I prayed. I leaned on my amazingly supportive husband, Rodney. That was a start, but more was needed! Here are four other things that I have done over the course of the past six years to survive (and THRIVE) in motherhood without having my mother:

1. Therapy is your friend - Postpartum depression is real! And many mothers don't tend to recognize it

when it happens. In my case, since I had already been experiencing some pretty sad days before giving birth, I was already in tune with my emotions, and I knew that I would be signing up for therapy once my son was born. It was the best decision ever!

2. Seeking out friendship and mentorship with older women/motherly figures - I have been blessed to have some awesome women step up and be there for me in huge ways over the years. Of course, no one could ever replace having my mother, but these women have truly encouraged me in ways they will never know! Like my Godmother, Deborah, whom I have known since I was in ninth grade. After the birth of my son, she flew to Chicago and stayed with us for three weeks cooking meals, helping with the baby, and just being a listening ear. My Aunt Helen has basically been my second mother my entire life. My stepmother Linda sadly passed away the year before my son was born, but before her passing, she was there for me for virtually every major milestone in my life from college until 2015 (even though she and my father divorced in the early nineties and she remarried in 2001, we remained connected and our bond was stronger than ever). Surrounding myself with women who genuinely love and care for me

and want God's best for my life has given me the confidence, strength, and wisdom I need to slay this motherhood thing!

3. Form your "Mom Squad" - Think of this as your A-Team (yes, I just dated myself)! This is the team of people that help keep you from losing your mind in the day-to-day throes of motherhood: nannies, parents, best friends, a cleaning service if you can spring one occasionally, your SPOUSE (get hubby involved and be as specific as possible with your wants and needs - men are NOT mind-readers). The idea is to ask for HELP and stop trying to be superwoman, and do everything yourself!

4. Give yourself credit! - One thing that I have noticed is that mothers are often judged harshly in today's society. And what's worse is that they are often judged harshly... by other mothers! You would think that we would overflow with grace and compassion for one another, but that is not always the case! Don't wait for anyone else's applause. If they give it, great. But if they do not, take a few moments before bed, look at yourself in the mirror, pat yourself on the back, and say, "You're doing amazing, sweetheart!" Release yourself from the pressures of "perfectly

curated for Instagram" motherhood. You've got this, Mama!

Bio

Nikeya Young is an Author/Certified Master Life Coach/Speaker, Licensed Minister, and Entertainer. A former educator with a Master's Degree in Special Education, and a B. A. in Psychology, Nikeya combines her gifts and talents, practical work experience, and spiritual gift of teaching to encourage others to live VICTORIOUSLY! She is passionate about empowering women and helping them discover their identity and God-given purpose. Nikeya is happily married to Rodney Young Jr and is a proud "Slay-at-Home," homeschooling mama bear to the couple's three beautiful children: Rodney III (R3) and twin baby girls Nalea and Nissi. The couple resides in the southern suburbs of Chicago, Illinois.

Chapter Twelve

Advocating for them to Save Me

Patrice Sterling

Would you say that every child deserves a champion? I would. Someone who advocates for them. That is, one who will fight or argue a cause on their behalf. Typically, the parent is the first person who comes to mind when we think of a child's support system. The one who will

go the extra mile. There's even an old saying I can remember hearing as I was growing up, mothers would say, "I don't play about mine," meaning their child. But what happens when that care and extra protection is motivated not only by love but by mean dark, grimy experiences? When the most normal question, like, can I stay the night with my friend, turns into an inquisition. What's the real motive behind the cringe when your child is innocently hugged by someone you know? And why does the mama bear come out when your child is asked a question that would probably not raise an eyebrow for most? You may be thinking, who does that? Me- I did.

So, a few years back, while completing an Advocacy training, the first question posed to the group consisted of only four words. Although only a few, those words were so powerful they forced me to take some time, dig deep and acknowledge the answer. The question? What is your why? As I gave thought to what really drives my position as an advocate, I became increasingly and (if I am honest) uncomfortably aware of the weight and why of its importance. I could easily say it is because my son was born with a chronic disease, and I want to help him and others like him. That would be a true statement, but to make it entirely true, I would have to recognize the fact that my advocacy for children started long before I thought of having my own. I realized that as a child, I never felt completely protected, and there were many times when I felt like most of the adults dropped the ball on my behalf. I never wanted to be that person, whether as an older friend or the other adult in the room. Don't get me wrong, there were beautiful times and wonderful opportunities for exposure, but when it was bad, it was really bad. From molestation to violent physical abuse, the outcomes of these types of traumas can be lifelong. For a long time, I was ashamed and silent. The thing about silence is it's a very effective way to keep victims quiet, but that doesn't make it right. It makes it inaudible and, at times, crippling. "Don't air your dirty laundry, or people will think less of you." Those are the words or something similar in vernacular I heard ringing inside my head again and again. The words are not only silencing but carry enormous burdens- burdens like guilt, hurt, and shame. I didn't want to embarrass my family. I didn't want friends to view me differently. Maybe the kids at school would find out. Fortunately, due to the uncertainty of not being protected, I was shaped into an independent advocate, first for myself and then for others. Again, I never wanted another child to feel this way.

Once I began having children, I wanted to make sure they always felt safe, loved, and supported. After all, no matter how old you are, financially stable, emotionally stable, religious background, or not, the desire for the reality that our parents are looking out for us is still there. Isn't that what we all want for our children? As a parent, my ultimate goal is to build in my kids the same strengths I never possessed as a kid. So, I spoke up for them when they couldn't, and I taught them to speak up for themselves as they grew.

Being a mom brings joy to my life. It's an honor and privilege to be there for them, to teach them, and to be a part of their lives. When I was pregnant with my first, I knew that being a mom would come with challenges. I was ready for the sleepless nights and diaper changes, but I wasn't ready for how much love I would have for her and my other children.

In order for a child to be grounded and feel secure and self-assured, that child needs to feel that its parents love them no matter what. That means you don't love them just because they're perfect, behave perfectly, or do everything you ever asked of them. The best way to give your child unconditional love is by being there for them when they need you—through good times and bad times—and not making things conditional on anything other than what's best for your child as an individual person. When you do this, your child will learn that his or her identity is separate from his or her behavior or achievements and that he or she is loved for who he or she is. Your child will feel secure in his or her own skin.

The greatest and most significant insight I gained from that one little question is that my love and ferociousness in advocating for my children was not just a result of the protection they needed but also a reflection of the protection I had longed for as a child. Each time I was there for them, healing took place within myself. In fact, advocating for them saved me.

To the moms who wonder if they're doing it right, if your kids are happy and healthy, you did good! When you become a parent, you have the opportunity to live life more fully than you ever have before. You can learn about yourself in the present and past through your children.

We are not our children. They have their own lives to live and their feelings to experience.

The first step is realizing that what has not healed within me will play out with them, whether they are young or adults. If there were traumas in your childhood that were not addressed, they would come up in some way in your relationship with your children. Just simply love them and yourself.

BIO

Patrice Sterling is an award-winning 2-time bestselling author. She is the CEO of Patrice Sterling Unlimited and Twenty-Two Publishing. She is a Sickle Cell Champion and Legislative Advocate, empowering families to find their voices, speak their truth and invoke the power of self-advocacy.

She knows the unique challenges all parents face and holds a special place in her heart for all those mothers wondering if they're missing the mark or doing right by their children. She hopes this project will impart good news- that while being a parent doesn't come with an instruction manual, you don't need one. You are enough, momma. By loving your child with your whole heart—especially on bad days—you're giving them exactly what they need; you.

Her greatest hope is to inspire others to find their space and stand firmly in it. If you want to tell your story, you can do it!

To work with Patrice, reach out to info@patricesterling.com.

Chapter Thirteen

There Is Honey in the Hard Places

Sonya Beavers

Who would have thought there would be honey in those hard places? Who would have ever imagined that those painful experiences that you went through would eventually bring you joy, fulfillment, happiness, etc. Do you remember the famous quote: "opposites attract?" Well, if my grandmother were alive today, she would say, "I beg to differ."

So, you mean to tell me that joy and pain, sunshine and rain, loss and gain, bliss and broken-heartedness, sorrow and happiness, life and death... these things attract? I think it is safe to say that if you have ever had to simultaneously deal with any of these mixed emotions, you know how powerfully yet painful your experiences can be.

For me, my experience began thirty years ago. Pregnant with twin boys. Ecstatic, excited, overjoyed, and thrilled at the fact that we would be adding not one but two additions to our growing family. We were living in great expectation of the day when our babies would make their grand entrance into the world. I was buying matching this and matching that, two of everything. Daydreaming constantly about my two babies. Thinking, what would they look like? What would their personalities be like? Imagining how precious they were going to be. Overjoyed whenever I felt the many kicks and watching my stomach grow by the day. Oh, the excitement and anticipation!

Until one day, life happened. The unexpected happened. It was April 2, 1992. I was six months into my pregnancy and went into the hospital for what I thought would be a routine prenatal appointment. To my surprise I ended up being admitted into Labor and Delivery as it was discovered that I was going into preterm labor. Tests showed that I was dilating, and they needed to stop it and stop it fast. My mind began to race, thoughts were everywhere, and panic began to set in. What was happening here? This cannot be! Yes, it was real and really happening!

Due to the fact that it was a multiple-birth pregnancy, the doctors were very attentive and concerned about my situation. They begin to run test, draw blood, and perform an ultrasound. The sonogram showed that I was experiencing what is called "Twin-to-Twin Transfusion Syndrome." This rare pregnancy condition affects identical twins or multiple birth pregnancies and can sometimes result in heart failure and death.

The doctors rushed to perform a procedure they hoped would save my twin baby that was in danger, and they told us that it was a 50/50 chance of him surviving. The next twenty-four hours were crucial. At first signs, the procedure went very well based on the sonogram. The doctors were ecstatic as they watched the twin who was once in distress now moving around and, as they said, turning flips. Moving forward, I was heavily monitored and treated for a few days. In the early morning of April 4th, around 5 am, I was awakened by a nurse asking me to drink a cup of cold water. She said the twins were moving around and needed to be located to get them back on the heart monitors. I drank the water, and she worked on my stomach for about five minutes and then suddenly left the room to return with three doctors who were moving very fast. I knew something was going on, as they were calm yet had very concerning looks on their faces. I asked, "Is everything ok?" After minutes of urgently rolling the transducer around my stomach, they looked at each other and then turned to me and said the dreaded words, "We are extremely sorry, but we've lost the heartbeat of one, and we don't know how sick the other baby is.""

Emergency cesarean surgery was performed at 9:04 am as my twin boys entered into this world. One survived, and one was stillborn. One alive and one deceased. One breathing and one immediately whisked away. As I lay on the operating table strapped down, feeling the tugging of my insides being worked on and feeling like I was going to lose my mind! I just remember saying, "Jesus... Jesus...Jesus... Jesus on repeat..." Over and over again.

All I could think about was, how can this be? What do I do next? How am I supposed to deal with life and death at the same time? How does a mother celebrate the birth of a child yet mourn losing one? My mind was racing, emotions were everywhere... feelings of joy and pain, loss and gain, grief and gladness. I didn't know which way to go, what to do, and where to turn. I literally thought that I was going to lose my mind. All I know is that it was God's grace that kept me. We're reminded in 2 Corinthians 12:9 that God's grace is sufficient. "My grace is sufficient for you, for My power is made perfect in your weakness." 2 Corinthians 12:9 And His word remains true. You see, God's plans are not like our plans. He is the Master Planner, and His plan are what prevails in the end. He will forever get the glory out of this situation even thirty years later. Every time I look at my healthy son, I am reminded of God's miraculous, wonderful works. Back then I didn't know the WHEN and the HOW of how He would one day use me to share my story, but here I am today being used as a testament to tell others that there is "Honey in the hard places". Just know that what seems hard in the moment will eventually prove that God purposed it for your good. What I thought would kill me only made me stronger and wiser. I didn't realize my own strength until it was tried and tested. I watched Him bring me out of that sad, depressing place of feeling guilty to a place of peace. I watched Him bring my baby, my surviving twin who once weighed one pound ten ounces to a healthy, smart, caring, athletic, kind, God-fearing, and now a loving thirty-year-old man. – Honey the Hard places.

So, I encourage you to embrace your journey with great joy, for there is purpose in your pain. Sometimes the honey is hard to detect when you are going through the storms of life, and you can't see your way out. So, when that happens, just remind yourself and hold on to the fact that there is HONEY in this. there is something sweet that is going to come out of this. Like honey in its natural state has staying power if it is sealed in an airtight vessel, it will last indefinitely, and it never spoils. So, like with us, the honey in those hard places will never spoil as it is sealed tight within our hearts and will be revealed in God's timing. BE BLESSED in your HONEY season(s).

Bio

Sonya Beavers is the Mother of 4 adult children, Myeisha, Laurice, Twin boys Akeem and Akele, and two grandchildren Carter, and Giselle.

She has a 25+ year financial/Administration career.

She is also a licensed life insurance agent/Financial Educator passionate about bringing financial literacy to marginalized communities.

She loves GOD and HIS people.

Chapter Fourteen

WHY DO I DO WHAT I DO
STEPHANIE SMITH

"Why do you do..." was the question asked various times since the day I found out I was pregnant. The answer is simple, yet complex, but necessary! I do... (this) because I have to. He is my only child, and if I don't invest in him, who will?

Over the last few years, the term "trauma" has been used loosely to define situations we may or may not have any control over. "Early childhood trauma generally refers to the traumatic experiences that occur to children aged 0-6." (NCTSN) Let me give you a few examples; if you have a parent who drinks: TRAUMA. If you are born to unmarried parents: TRAUMA. If you are low income: TRAUMA. If you have a parent who is a convicted felon: TRAUMA. These traumas can cause developmental delays, misbehaving in school, etcetera. I am not disputing that the term is not relevant nor important, but for me, with my "fancy education and all," I am determined not to have my son become another statistic. He had those traumas listed and some stacked against him from Day Zero. At four, while driving to the daycare, my son says, "Mommy, it's just {name} and mommy, I don't have a daddy!" My response to him was simple: "{Name}, you do have a daddy; he's just not here; he's at work." I did not lie: TRAUMA.

As an educator, and a single black female, I knew firsthand how my son could possibly be treated, especially with the more recent events of police brutality, and I felt obligated to pour into my son wholeheartedly.

When I found out that I was pregnant, it was not the best circumstances nor what I had hoped for. However, I didn't let that change the fact that I was about to become a mother. I knew he was mine, and I was his mommy. I mean, I had carried him for eight plus months. When the doctor first introduced us, my first reply was, "Put him back, put him back; he looks too much like his dad!" When he first started talking/babbling, his first sound was "da, da, da, da, da." I took offense naturally because, I mean, I literally grew his ears.

I took advantage of every opportunity that came my way. The weekly class gave a pack of diapers, an hour class for a car seat, an hour for a playpen, as well as the classes that teach you how to bathe a baby, nurse, etc. I was overloaded with information. I had an application or email describing everything to expect up until the first year. I utilized every resource available to me, especially what was free. I filled out the recall form for every toy I brought or was given.

I make sure that I use my fancy education for something when it comes to my son. When he started crawling, I posted only his name and birthdate throughout the house. I recited the alphabet during every diaper change and was excited at the letters in his initials. As he started walking, I posted the numbers one through ten on the wall, and we would count as he went up the stairs. I would narrate to him when I bathed him or walked to check the mail. Now at five, I am told what is what instead of getting asked why questions. Oftentimes, I have to remind him that he is a child. His reply, "I am not a child. I am {Name}!"

Sure, there were and still are plenty of times that I wanted to cry with and for him, and I have and will. But I will say God definitely gifted this child to me and has given me the strength even when I could barely keep my eyes open. He was a delayed speaker (per his doctor): TRAUMA. But my faith wouldn't allow this. My son is my first and only living birth, and again I pour into him because I know that if I don't, it will affect every ramification of his life. I followed all speech requirements, and he was literally kicked out/graduated within six to eight months.

I made sure that I taught my son that he was a brown boy. He knows, "I'm a brown boy, and mommy is a brown girl." His family service worker asked, "Why did you teach him that?" My reply was, "No matter how smart he is, how good he is at playing basketball, how polite he is, at the end of the day, he is still a brown boy that will be judged by the color of his skin. And to me, it is important that he knows who he is." Her response was, "Wow, I didn't realize that these conversations have to be had."

I have had a significant amount of help with my son (family and friends, both near and far, church, and daycare), and I am grateful to each and every person who answered my questions or told me off the ledge when I was being too extreme with worrying. My faith and trust in God with this precious gift that he gave me to raise is so strong that I can't mess this up, regardless of any traumas he may or may not have. I don't claim negative outcomes, especially concerning his life. I make a point to tell my son that I am proud of him and talk to him like a human being. My ultimate goal is to raise a functional adult; regardless of what life throws our way, we will surpass and continue to be blessed.

My advice to any mother, especially a new mother: there is absolutely NO manual for how to deal with every situation that will come (potty training, sickness, bug bites, etc.), and there will be plenty of moments where being the adult SUCKS, but remember God gave this gift to you. Cherish the moments, enjoy the meltdowns, put your phone down, and focus on your child.

"Early Childhood Trauma." The National Child Traumatic Stress Network (NCTSN). Retrieved on June 27, 2022, from https://www.nctsn.org/what-is-child-trauma/trauma-types/early-childhood-trauma

Bio

Originally from Lynchburg, Virginia, Stephanie Smith spent her early career working in fast food management before transitioning into education.

Stephanie says the best part of what she does is building rapport with students, hands down. She is passionate about finding innovative ways to help students use what they already know and apply it to mathematical concepts. She is currently a mathematical Academic Instructor with a knack for storytelling and clear explanations.

She is a Christian. She is an educator. But most importantly, she is a mother. For more than ten years, she has helped many find ways to work smarter, not harder.

She can be reached by email at carameldq7@gmail.com

Chapter Fifteen

IT ISN'T ABOUT YOU ANYMORE, GIRL!

Takeallah Rivera

Hearing these words constantly as an expectant mother felt like I had been hit with a ton of bricks. I was twenty-three, heartbroken, and had recently spent thirty-six hours on a Greyhound bus with no food or money after my son's father decided that I, the relationship, and our unborn child were "too much." He sent me back to Memphis, Tennessee, from Spokane, Washington, without even as much as a "Goodbye." When I stepped off the Greyhound bus in Memphis, I collapsed into my mother's arms in tears and let out a sigh of relief and exhaustion. I knew that I had a tough road ahead of me as a single mother, but I was adamant about carrying my pregnancy to term and parenting my child. I spent the pregnancy on my mother's couch, perusing books, articles, and websites on everything about parenting during the day and choking back my tears at night. As my pregnancy progressed, I began to notice that the tears and negative feelings were not fading away, as family and friends had promised me several times- they were increasing. Whenever I tried to discuss my feelings with my family members, I was almost always brushed off, told to "put on my big girl panties," or told, "you are about to be a mother. It's not about you anymore!" Eventually, I stopped reaching out to family and friends about my feelings and began to suppress them, only revealing my true emotions to the journal I kept underneath my mother's couch. One morning after a crying spell, I googled my symptoms and came across an assessment on maternal depression and anxiety. As I read through each question, I nodded my head in agreement. I grabbed my AmeriGroup Member Handbook, searched for the closest mental health provider, and scheduled an appointment with a clinician. At my clinic, I fidgeted with the straps of my handbag as I anxiously awaited my turn with the clinician.

During my appointment, I discussed the past year's events with the clinician and my current symptoms- the crying spells, the crippling feelings of hopelessness and impending doom, insomnia, and chronic fatigue. After taking extensive notes, the clinician diagnosed me with Panic Disorder, Major Depressive Disorder, and Post Traumatic Stress Syndrome and recommended pregnancy-safe antidepressants and talk therapy. My diagnosis came as no surprise to me, and I was eager to start treatment and finally begin prioritizing my mental health. After my appointment, I went home, grabbed my journal from under the couch, and began to map out a Self-Care Plan to improve my symptoms in preparation for my son's arrival.

On my path to healing, I began to walk two to three miles per day, journal twice a day, spend time reading and writing short stories, and take my medication as prescribed. I began to feel better and started to smile once more. However, I noticed that the more I focused on my happiness and mental health, the more criticisms I began to receive from family, friends, and strangers. I was often met with disparaging remarks attacking my motherhood. "All you think about is yourself- that shows what kind of mother you are going to be!" "You're so selfish! What are you going to do when that baby gets here?" "It isn't about you anymore! Time to step up and be a real woman!" The internalized misogynoir, constant rejection, and cruel remarks motivated me to leave the environment I was in and make my dream of relocating a reality. I was determined to raise my son in a positive, healthy environment, free from the toxicity I had been subjected to my entire life.

When my son was seven months, I received an offer to serve as an AmeriCorps member in Seattle, Washington. With two packed bags and my purse, I boarded a plane in early January with my young son in search of positive change and new opportunities. Within a month, I was settled into my work as a Food Access Coordinator, and my son was settled into his new daycare. We were comfortable in our new two-bedroom apartment, and I was taking advantage of every professional and educational opportunity that fell into my lap. From that point forward, I focused on tackling the goals I had written out during my pregnancy and displaying happiness, positivity, and ambition to my son. We spent our time in the Pacific Northwest exploring nature, trying new foods, attending art shows and concerts, and traveling.

Over the years, I watched my son grow from a curious infant into a vivacious young man while I simultaneously grew past my traumas and into the woman and mother I always desired to be. My commitment to modeling self-preservation and prioritizing mental health has resulted in raising a son who is self-aware, empathetic, and communicative about his needs. I pride myself on having a son who is comfortable saying, "Mom, I am struggling with this. Can you please help me?" And "Mom, I am feeling very overwhelmed today. Can I take a mental health day and rest?" I encourage every mother who has been told, "It isn't about you anymore!" To eliminate this phrase from your memory bank because it is simply not the truth. Motherhood is about you. It is about your mental health, happiness, needs, wants, goals, and dreams. Your babies are watching you and will grow up to model what you have shown them. So, take the time to speak with your therapist regularly, hire a babysitter Saturday night and catch up with your girlfriends over drinks. Place room in your budget for that Pilates membership you have been longing for, and take a few hours of Paid Time Off while the kids are in school to get a deluxe pedicure and take yourself to lunch. Take care of yourself because **it is always about you.**

Bio

Takeallah Rivera is a Cool, Millennial Mom, Full Spectrum Doula, Lactation Educator, Childbirth Educator, and a dedicated Reproductive Justice and Maternal Mental Health advocate. Takeallah works from a trauma-informed and healing-centered lens to improve maternal health outcomes in marginalized communities.

She is currently pursuing a Bachelor of Arts Science in Therapeutic Use of Adventure Education, a Certification in Mindfulness Teaching, and a Certification in Pregnancy, Postpartum, and Baby Nutrition.

In her spare time, she enjoys studying astrology, practicing yoga, krav maga, meditation, and exploring the horror movie genre. Takeallah resides in Memphis, TN, with her two children, Racquel and Hendrix.

Chapter Sixteen

My Mom Truth

Tosin Ola

I never thought I would be a mom... and I don't think I'm a great mom. But I am the best mom for my twins, and I was meant to be their mom.

I was born with an inherited rare disease called sickle cell hemoglobin SS anemia. A long mouthful, so we'll call it SCD. My bone marrow produces defective red blood cells (sickled cells) that stick together and don't carry enough oxygen. They clump and block circulation to vital tissues and organs throughout my body, leading to painful clots, frequent hospital/ER visits, and end-organ damage. As of 2022, the

CDC puts the average lifespan of a female with SCD at forty-two to forty-six years old. I decided to live my very best 'short' life and enjoy every moment I could.

At four, the Nigerian physician diagnosed me. He told my parents not to waste money on my education since I probably wouldn't live past childhood. They brought me to America to give me a better chance at survival. Due to chronic anemia, constant fatigue, unexpected flare-ups, excruciating pain, and the daunting reality of SCD, US doctors told me there was a slim chance I could ever be pregnant or successfully carry to term.

As I grew, I experienced more frequent pain episodes, sometimes every other month, lasting for days or weeks. SCD was the uninvited gatecrasher at every special family or social event. We would be having a great time, and in the next hour, my parents were rushing me to the hospital. The pain felt like 1,000 men with jackhammers drilling into my body.

My OBGYN told me that since I was the only one with SCD, I could single-handedly eradicate this disease in my bloodline by not having kids at all.

Children always seemed drawn to me. I didn't hate kids, but I really saw no value or purpose to them beyond progeny, an ego boost, or gross inconvenience. Sure, for money or a close friend, I could babysit here and there. During my gap year before college, I even had a job at a preschool/daycare where I was amazed at the school-aged kids. But babies, no way. I didn't like their drool, mess, innate helplessness, inability to talk, and all the effort required to keep them alive. I figured I would settle with being the cool aunt who always gave the babies back.

At twenty-one, I was a college graduate working as a cardiac nurse 2,000 miles away from home. I was adulting; with my own townhouse and fat paychecks, I couldn't spend fast enough. I traveled, shopped, partied, and was living my best life. I met Dick (fake Name), and we got together. He was a nurse and veteran and seemed to check all the boxes. We had sex a handful of times, and one day he failed to tell me the condom broke.

At first, I thought I was having the world's longest period - twenty-one days. It wasn't until the morning when I had huge plum-sized clots coming out, that I was scared enough to go to the ER. Twenty minutes after I found out I was pregnant; I was told I was experiencing a spontaneous miscarriage at seven weeks. Dick was brutally mean when I called him to tell him we were pregnant. He yelled at me, refused to come to the hospital, and told me to get rid of 'it.' The doctors told me I had bled out the baby, and sometimes miscarriages just happen with no explanation. I remember sobbing my eyes out in that lonely hospital room, terrified and sad over a baby I didn't even know I wanted until it was no longer possible. I took a cab home the following morning and didn't hear from Dick for three days. Needless to say, we broke up.

My tears turned to an icy wall inside my chest. I was grieving. I got the message from Mother Nature that, for me, it was just never meant to be. I protected myself the only way I could, with anger, then outright derision. I joined the "Live Childfree" society, scorned those with "ankle-biters," avoided all my pregnant friends, and never cooed over any baby. I skipped baby showers and birthday parties. I told myself I would never be one of those tired, stressed-out moms; it just seemed like a lot of extra work with minimal payout. When coworkers brought their baby in for show-n-tell, I would feign interest, then casually beeline for the snacks and leave quickly. I didn't have to think about diapers, car seats, bottles, Legos, binkies, or college tuition. I could spend my money as I liked, go wherever I pleased, and go bungee-jumping without a life insurance policy.

Fast forward to meeting the right guy, getting married, and planning our future. He shared custody of a son already from his first marriage, so he was okay with my Childfree plan. We went skydiving to celebrate our first wedding anniversary. On days off, we slumbered until noon, ordered pizza, and stayed in bed playing video games all day. We stopped using condoms because I knew I couldn't get pregnant. We were jet-setting, in love, young, spontaneous, energetic, and daring.

When I hit thirty-one, suddenly, my hormones broke through the ice wall. Mother Nature roared and could not be denied. I had babies on my mind all the freaking time. I would grab him and beg, "Put a baby in me, right now!" We practiced every chance we could, exploring tantra, unusual positions, herbs, and all our fantasies. We kept practicing daily and even hit the jackpot a few times. Each sadly ended in miscarriages, another slew of tears, another plum-sized clot in the toilet, triggered again by my body, genes, SCD, God, or Mother Nature. I was a miscarriage pro at this point. I dealt with the 4th one all by myself, "I guess it's not meant to be," I said as I buried what was left of my motherhood dreams with the tissue I had expelled from my body. After the 5th miscarriage, I told Orion the chapter was closed and dusted off my Childfree card. We were done baby-making. My heart, body, soul, and mind just couldn't take the heartbreak and disappointment anymore.

The Yoruba people are the most fertile folks to have twins naturally. We believe that twins are a blessing, a good omen.

If you take good care of them, you will be blessed by your ancestors. If you mistreat them, calamity will befall you.

Surprisingly four years later, my natural, unplanned twin pregnancy was our miraculous rainbow gift. I found the best high-risk OBGYN in the county. I was determined to let them stay in the womb and "cook" as long as possible, no matter what sacrifices I had to make for my body. Instead of parasailing, my anniversary adventure that year was waiting in wonder, fear, and anticipation, worried that one of us wouldn't make it. After sixty-five hospitalized days of specialized medical interventions (twenty-one units of blood, two blood exchange transfusions, and one baby shower in the visitor's lounge), we made it. My twelve-hour labor and delivery felt like mild cramps compared to my usual SCD crisis pain. Thankfully they arrived naturally at 38.5 weeks, which for twins is full-term.

With kids, every day is a new adventure, just waiting to be explored. Your children come to you already perfect. Any challenges or conflict that exists with them is actually allowing you to look closer at yourself. You must give them the tools to cope and exist independently in this world; however, you cannot live their lives for them.

Drop the pressure. Kids are not meant to be mini-yous or your attempt to clone your failed wishes and dreams. They come knowing the life they are meant to lead. Your job is to nourish them to achieve their purpose. Our kids learn more from what we do than what we say. You can correct the family dysfunction in your generational bloodline and help break the chains that hold the family down. Effective communication, trust, and mutual respect are key to every successful relationship, even a parent-child one.

I tell my boys when I'm having a hard day. I apologize when I mess up. I talk about my emotions and challenges, showing my human side. I share when I'm angry and talk about what's going on in my head so they learn better-coping strategies. By expressing my boundaries, I teach them to honor themselves and others' boundaries.

The best teacher of life's lessons and beauty is a child. Do not crush their souls. They are all wonderfully perfect. Nourish and magnify that light.

BIO

Tosin Ola, RN, BSN, MSN a practicing registered nurse and mother of twins, launched the Sickle Cell Blog and coined the term "sickle cell warrior" in 2005. Her words shifted the dynamics of the provider-patient relationship, restoring dignity, strength, and respect in situations where one is often most vulnerable.

In 2007, Ms. Ola created and is the Editor-in-Chief for the Sickle Cell Warriors, Inc website. Ms. Ola created a portal of connection and community where there was none, with over 26,000 warriors globally, making it the most prominent online group of people affected by SCD.

Tosin is an authoritative speaker for radio shows & podcasts, interviewed for print publications like ESSENCE, Glamour, and Minority Nurse; authored content in online media like the New York Times, U.S. News & World Report, EveryNurse, WEGOHealth, Wellsphere, and many more.

Tosin lives in San Diego, California, with her 8-year-old twins and husband. Visit the Sickle Cell Warriors website or email Tosin directly at Tosin@SickleCellWarriors.com.

www.ingramcontent.com/pod-product-compliance
Lightning Source LLC
Chambersburg PA
CBHW041453010526
44107CB00013B/1032